A Trip to London

I Talk You Talk Press

CONTENTS

INTRODUCTION

The words in **bold** are useful travel phrases.

You might hear these phrases, and you can use some of these phrases when you travel.

David Wang is a university student from Shanghai. He is twenty years old. He studies English at university.

It is August. He is travelling to the UK. He wants to visit many places and he wants to practice his English. He also wants to make many new friends. He is very excited. It is his first time to leave China and go to another country.

1. ON THE AEROPLANE

Now, David is on the aeroplane. He is sitting next to the window. He is looking out of the window. The sky is blue and the clouds below look soft and white. It is beautiful. He takes his camera out of his bag and takes a photograph.

"Excuse me sir, would you like something to drink?"

He turns around. The flight attendant is looking at him.

"Yes please," he says.

"What would you like?"

"Can I have an orange juice please?" he asks.

"Here you are," says the flight attendant.

"Thank you," says David. He drinks the orange juice. It is very sweet. He looks at his watch. He will arrive in the UK in eight hours. He closes his eyes and goes to sleep.

He wakes up. He can smell food. He looks around. No one is eating. He feels hungry.

He looks at the man next to him. The man is reading a book.

"Excuse me," says David.

The man looks at him and smiles.

"Yes?"

"When is dinner served?"

"Dinner? We just finished dinner. You were asleep," says the man.

"Oh, I see. I'm very hungry," says David. He is worried. Maybe he can't have dinner!

The man points to a button on David's seat. "You can call the flight attendant. She will bring your dinner," he says.

"Oh, thank you," says David.

David presses the button. A flight attendant comes. She smiles.

"Yes, sir, how can I help you?"

"I'd like some dinner, please," says David. "I was asleep."

"Yes, of course. Would you like chicken or fish?"

"Chicken, please," says David.

Please wait a moment," says the flight attendant. She brings a tray.

"Here you are sir," she says.

"Thank you," says David.

He looks at the tray. There is some water, a small salad, a small chocolate cake, some cheese and crackers, and a hot dish. He opens the hot dish. There is some chicken and many potatoes and carrots. He eats his dinner. It is not so delicious, but he is hungry, so he eats everything.

"Would you like tea or coffee, sir?" asks the flight attendant.

"Coffee, please," he says.

"Milk and sugar?" asks the flight attendant.

"Just sugar, please," he says. He drinks the coffee. It is strong and bitter.

He looks around the plane. Some people are sleeping. Other people are reading books, or watching movies. He puts his earphones on and listens to music. After an hour, he falls asleep again.

2. AT IMMIGRATION

David gets off the plane and walks into Heathrow Airport. He goes to immigration. He has to fill in a landing card. He writes his name, address, date of birth, passport number, and nationality. Then, he has trouble. There is a word - occupation. He doesn't understand. *What is occupation?*

He looks around. There is a woman standing next to him.

"Excuse me," he says.

"Yes?" says the woman.

"Could you help me, please? I don't understand occupation," says David.

"Occupation means *job*," says the woman.

"Oh, I see. Thank you," says David.

He writes 'student'. Then, he stands in line and waits.

"Next!"

He goes to the immigration counter.

The immigration officer is a woman.

"Show me your passport and landing card, please," she says.

David gives her his passport and landing card.

"Where are you from?" she asks.

"I'm from Shanghai in China," says David.

"What is the purpose of your visit to the UK?" she asks.

"Pardon?" David doesn't understand. The woman is speaking very fast.

"What is the purpose of your visit? Why did you come here?"

she asks.

"Oh, I see. Sightseeing," says David.

"How long will you be staying?" she asks.

"I will be staying for a week," says David.

"And where will you be staying?"

"I will be staying at a hotel in London," says David.

The woman stamps his passport.

"OK, here you are," she says.

"Thank you," says David.

David walks to the baggage reclaim area. He waits for his suitcase. Many people are waiting for their suitcases. Many suitcases come, but David cannot see his suitcase. After ten minutes, he starts to feel worried. *Where is my suitcase?* He waits, and waits, but his suitcase does not come.

He goes to the baggage counter and says to the woman at the counter **"Excuse me, my suitcase hasn't arrived."**

"Which flight were you on?" asks the woman.

"The flight from Shanghai," says David.

"OK, let me check…" says the woman. She checks her computer.

"Your suitcase is here in London. Please wait a few more minutes. It will come soon."

"OK, thank you," says David.

There are three other people waiting for their suitcases, too.

Then, after twenty minutes, he sees his suitcase.

He smiles. "My suitcase!"

He takes his suitcase and walks out into the airport arrival hall. He looks around. The airport is very big and there are many people. He sees a sign for the taxi rank. He walks outside. It is August, but it is not so hot. It is cool. He finds a taxi.

3. IN THE TAXI

David looks at his hotel information sheet.

"I'd like to go to the Park Hotel, please," he says to the driver.

"The Park Hotel? OK," says the driver.

David sits in the taxi and looks out of the window. There are many cars on the road. The sky is grey.

The taxi stops outside a hotel. "This is the Park Hotel," says the driver.

"How much is the fare?" asks David.

"It's fifty pounds," says the driver.

"Here you are," says David. He gives the driver the money. He picks up his suitcase and walks into the hotel.

4. AT CHECK-IN

"**Good evening sir,**" says the receptionist.

"**Good evening. I have a reservation. My name is David Wang,**" says David.

The receptionist looks at her computer.

"**Oh yes, Mr Wang. I have your reservation here. Welcome to the Park Hotel. Could you fill in this check-in form, please?**"

David picks up a pen and writes his name and address.

"**Could I see your passport, please?**" asks the receptionist.

"**Yes, here you are,**" says David.

"**Thank you. Your room is number 302. This is your room key,**" says the receptionist.

"**Thank you. What time is breakfast in the morning?**" asks David.

"**Breakfast is served from seven o clock to ten o clock in the restaurant,**" says the receptionist.

"**OK, thank you,**" says David.

David gets into the elevator and goes up to the third floor. He finds room 302 and opens the door. It is very dark. He presses the light switch, but the lights don't work. He opens the curtains.

Why don't the lights work? he thinks.

He sees a telephone next to the bed. The number for the reception desk is 0. He dials 0 and the receptionist answers.

"**Hello, this is the reception desk, Lisa speaking,**" says the receptionist.

"**Hello. This is David Wang in room 302,**" says David.

"**Hello, Mr Wang. How can I help you?**" says Lisa.

"**The lights don't work. It's very dark,**" says David.

"**Oh, I'm sorry Mr Wang. I forgot to tell you. On the wall next to the door, there is a slot for your room key. When you put the room key in the slot on the wall, the lights will work,**" says Lisa.

"**Oh, I see, thank you,**" says David.

He puts the key into the slot on the wall, and all the lights come on. It is very bright!

David feels hungry. He looks at the room service menu, but it is very expensive. He looks at the hotel restaurant menu. That is very expensive, too. He is very tired. He doesn't want to go to a restaurant. He looks out of the window. There is a small shop.

David goes to the shop. In the shop, there are many sandwiches, sweets, cakes, drinks, and other things. He buys a packet of sandwiches, a bottle of fruit juice and some chocolate.

He goes back to his hotel room and eats his dinner. Then, he has a bath. He feels very sleepy. He goes to bed at 9:00pm and dreams about his trip.

5. BREAKFAST

The next morning, David wakes up at 6:30am. He feels very relaxed and refreshed. He opens the curtains. It is sunny and the sky is light blue. He switches the TV on and changes the channel to BBC. He watches the BBC news and the weather forecast. It will be sunny today and tomorrow. He feels very happy.

At 7:00am he gets in the lift and goes down to the ground floor. He walks into the restaurant.

"Good morning sir," says the waiter.

"Good morning," says David.

He sits down at a table.

The waiter comes to his table.

"Breakfast is self-service. We have a breakfast buffet. Please help yourself," says the waiter.

"OK, thank you," says David.

David goes to the long breakfast buffet table. He picks up a plate. There are many dishes. There are eggs, bacon, sausages, toast, bread, mushrooms, tomatoes, beans, yogurt, fruit, cereal, juice, tea and coffee. He takes an egg, some bacon, mushrooms and toast, and a glass of orange juice. He sits down and eats his breakfast. It is delicious. Then, he goes back to the buffet and takes a yogurt and a grapefruit and some coffee. He looks around the restaurant. There are many people. Some people are tourists and some people are businessmen and businesswomen. The people are speaking many languages. He hears French, Russian and Korean.

He looks at his guidebook. Today, he will visit Big Ben and other famous sights in London. He is very excited.

After breakfast, he goes to the reception desk.

"Good morning Mr Wang, how can I help you?" asks Lisa.

"How can I get from here to the centre of London? I'd like to go to Big Ben," says David.

"OK. You can take the bus or taxi. The bus is cheaper, but it takes longer. The taxi is quicker, but it's more expensive," says Lisa.

"I'll take the bus," says David. **"Where can I get on the bus?"**

"There is a bus stop outside the hotel. You need bus number fourteen."

"How long does it take to get to the centre?"

"It takes about thirty minutes," says Lisa.

"OK, thank you," says David.

"You're welcome," says Lisa. **"Have a good day!"**

6. ON THE BUS

David waits for the bus. A bus comes. It is a number five bus.

No, not this bus, he thinks. *I need bus number…oh! What number? Ah, number forty! Yes, number forty!* He sees bus number forty and he gets on the bus.

"To the centre, please," says Wang to the driver.

"The centre? This bus doesn't go to the centre," says the driver.

"Really?" says David.

"Yes. You need bus number fourteen, not bus number forty," says the driver.

"Oh, I see," says David. He gets off the bus and waits. A number fourteen bus comes and he gets on it.

"How much is it to the centre?" he asks the driver.

"It's three pounds twenty please," says the driver. David pays and takes his ticket.

He sits down next to the window.

He looks around the bus.

How do I get off the bus? he thinks.

At the next stop, he watches an old woman get off the bus. She presses the stop button near her seat, and the driver stops at the next bus stop.

Thirty minutes later, he arrives in the centre of London. He stands up and presses the stop button near his seat. The bus stops and he gets off.

7. SIGHTSEEING AND MAKING A NEW FRIEND

David walks around the centre of London. He walks for many hours and takes many photographs. Then, he sees a red double-decker bus. The bus is an open-top sightseeing bus. Many people are sitting on the top floor of the bus and enjoying a sightseeing tour.

"That's a good idea!" he says. He wants to take the sightseeing bus.

A man is standing next to him. The man is a tourist.

"Excuse me," says David. **"I'd like to take that sightseeing bus tour. Where can I buy a ticket?"**

"I'd like to take the tour, too. We can buy tickets over there, at the tourist information office. Shall we go together?" says the man.

"Yes, OK," says David. The man and David walk across the road.

"Where are you from?" asks David.

"I'm from Kenya," says the man. "How about you?"

"I'm from China," says David. "Nice to meet you. I'm David."

"Nice to meet you, too. I'm Gary."

David and Gary go into the tourist information office.

"Good morning, gentlemen, how can I help you?" says the man in the tourist information office.

"We would like to go on the bus tour," says David. **"How much is it?"**

"It is twenty-six pounds," says the man.

"How long is the tour?" asks Gary.

"It lasts two hours and a half in total," says the man. **"But, the**

ticket is a twenty-four hour ticket, so you can get on and off the bus anytime in the next twenty-four hours. Would you like to pay separately or together?"

"Separately please," says David.

"OK, that's twenty-six pounds each, please," says the man.

David and Gary pay. The man gives them their tickets.

"The next bus will come very soon. It will leave from the bus stop over there," says the man.

"Thank you very much," say David and Gary.

The bus comes and they get on. There are many other tourists on the bus. David and Gary sit together at the back.

The tour guide's name is Sandra. She is very friendly and she knows many things about London. The tour goes to Buckingham Palace, The Tower of London, Downing Street, Big Ben and many other places. David and Gary take many photographs and David takes a video.

The tour finishes. They get off the bus.

"Are you hungry?" asks Gary.

"Yes, I am," says David.

"Shall we have lunch together?" asks Gary.

"Yes, that would be nice," says David.

They go into a restaurant and order lunch. Gary has pie and chips and David has chicken and potatoes. It is very delicious.

"How long are you staying in London, David?" asks Gary.

"I'm staying here for a week," says David. "How about you?"

"I've been here for a week. Tomorrow, I'm going to Paris," says Gary.

"In the future, I'd like to go to Paris," says David.

"Yes, it's a very nice city," says Gary.

After lunch, they ask the waiter for the bill. The waiter brings the bill.

David opens his bag and takes out his wallet. Gary looks in his bag.

"Where is my wallet? I can't find my wallet!" says Gary.

Gary and David look in Gary's bag, but they cannot find his wallet.

"Perhaps I left it on the bus," says Gary. "I opened my bag to take out my camera. Perhaps my wallet fell out of my bag onto the bus floor."

"I'll pay for lunch here," says David. "Then, we can go to the tourist information centre and ask the information centre staff about your wallet."

"Oh, thank you, David. You are very kind," says Gary.

"You're welcome," says David.

David pays and they walk back to the tourist information centre.

"Excuse me. I think I left my wallet on the bus," says Gary. **"Could you check with the tour guide, please?"**

"I'll check with the tour guide when the tour finishes," says the man. "Now, the tour guide will be very busy."

David looks outside.

"Oh look! It's the bus!" says David.

Gary looks outside. The bus is just stopping.

"Run!" says David.

They run outside and get on the bus just as it is leaving. They run up the stairs to the top floor and go to the back of the bus. There are many people on the bus.

A man and a woman are sitting on the seat at the back.

"Excuse me, may I look under the seat, please?" asks David. "My friend has lost his wallet."

"Yes, of course," says the woman.

David and Gary look under the seat.

"There it is! My wallet!" says Gary. He picks his wallet up off the floor.

"That's lucky!" says David.

"Yes, it is," says Gary. He takes some money out of his wallet and gives it to David.

"This is for lunch. Thank you for paying for me," says Gary.

David takes the money and puts it in his wallet.

"No problem," says David.

"Oh look! The next stop is the London Eye! Shall we go on it?" asks Gary.

"Yes! That sounds great!" says David.

They get off the bus and go to the London Eye.

They have to wait for a long time to get tickets. They get into a capsule. There are twenty other people in the capsule. They stand at the window. From the top, they can see across London. The view is wonderful. David and Gary take many photographs.

"Let's get a photograph of us together," says Gary.

"Yes, that's a good idea," says David.

There is a woman standing next to them.

"Excuse me," says David. **"Could you take a photograph of me and my friend, please?"**

"Sure," says the woman. David gives her his camera and she takes a photo of Gary and David. Then, Gary gives her his camera and she takes a photo with Gary's camera.

"Thank you very much," says David.

"You're welcome," says the woman. "Where are you from?"

"I'm from China, and my friend is from Kenya," says David. "Are you from England?"

"No, I'm not. I'm from Scotland," says the woman. "Have you been to Scotland?"

"No, I haven't. But I hope I can go sometime," says David.

Thirty minutes later, they get off the London Eye. They get back on the bus and go back to the tourist information office.

"I had a really good time today. Thank you, David," says Gary.

"I had a good time, too," says David. "Let's keep in touch. This is my email address."

"Yes, let's do that. Here is my email address," says Gary. "Please come to Kenya someday. I will take you sightseeing."

"Thank you. I hope you can come to China someday. I will take you sightseeing in Shanghai," says David.

"Great! I hope I can visit you someday," says Gary.

They shake hands and David gets the bus back to his hotel. He is very happy. He had a good day sightseeing, he spoke lots of English and he made a new friend.

8. GOING TO THE BANK AND GOING SHOPPING

The next day, David wakes up at 6:00am. He looks out of the window. The sky is grey, and it is raining. He decides to go shopping. He has to buy some souvenirs for his friends and family.

First, he needs to draw some money out of his bank account. He goes to the bank. There are many cash machines. He has never used an English cash machine before. He reads the screen instructions.

"Please insert your card."

He inserts his card.

"Enter your PIN number."

He enters his PIN number.

"Options - Cash, Cash with receipt, Balance on screen, Printed balance, Print statement, Change PIN."

He chooses "Cash with receipt."

"Select amount."

He selects £100.

"Please wait. Your cash is being counted."

He waits.

"Please remove your card."

He removes his card.

"Please remove your cash."

He removes his cash and puts it in his wallet.

"Please remove your receipt."

He removes his receipt.

Then, he walks out of the bank.

David finds a souvenir shop. There are many souvenirs - books, postcards, T-shirts, bookmarks, badges, caps, hats, pens, key rings and many, many other items.

"Can I help you?" asks the shop assistant.

"Yes, I'd like to buy some T-shirts," says David. "I like this blue T-shirt."

"What size would you like?" asks the shop assistant.

"I'm not sure. Can I try it on?" asks David.

"Yes, we have a fitting room over there," says the shop assistant.

David tries on a medium-sized T shirt. It fits perfectly.

"I'll take two of these T-shirts. One in blue and one in white," says David.

"I'm sorry, sir. We have sold out of white T-shirts in your size. How about this red T-shirt?"

"Oh, I see. Yes, I'll take a blue one and a red one. How much are they?" asks David.

"They are ten pounds each, or three for twenty pounds," says the shop assistant.

"Pardon?" David doesn't understand.

"It's a special offer. If you buy three, you only pay twenty pounds," says the shop assistant.

"Oh, I see. OK, I'll take two blue ones and a red one," says David.

David looks at the souvenirs. He buys some pens, pencils, and postcards for his friends, and a book, a cap, some biscuits, some jam, some tea and a picture of London Bridge for his mother and father.

"That's fifty pounds please," says the shop assistant. **"How would you like to pay?"**

"In cash, please," says David.

He pays and leaves the shop. The bag is heavy. **"I hope I have room in my suitcase!"** says David.

It is raining very hard, so David spends the day in a museum. The museum is very big and after a few hours he feels tired. He decides to stop for lunch at a pub. It is his first time to go to an English pub.

9. IN THE PUB

He walks into the pub. He finds an empty table and sits down. There is a menu on the table. He looks at the menu. There are many dishes. He chooses a fish pie and vegetables. He looks for a waiter. There are no waiters.

How do I order? he thinks.

He asks a couple sitting at the next table.

"Excuse me, how do I order?" he asks.

"Your table has a number. Go to the bar and tell the bar man your table number and order your food and drink. Then, pay for your meal, and take your drink," says the woman.

"I see. Thank you," says David.

He looks at his table number. It is number eight. He goes to the bar.

"Yes, sir, what would you like?" says the bar man.

"Can I order some food please?" asks David.

"Sure. What's your table number?" asks the bar man.

"Number eight," says David.

"OK. What would you like?" asks the man.

"Can I have a fish pie please?" asks David.

"OK. Would you like chips or mashed potatoes with your pie?" asks the bar man.

"Er…mashed potatoes please," says David.

"What would you like to drink?" asks the bar man.

David looks at the drinks. There are so many drinks! He decides to try an English beer.

"**What English beer do you recommend?**" he asks.

"**I recommend bitter,**" says the bar man.

"**OK, I will have that,**" says David.

"**Would you like a pint or half a pint?**" asks the bar man.

"**A pint, please,**" says David.

"**OK, one moment please,**" says the bar man.

The bar man gives David his drink.

"**That is twelve pounds, please,**" says the bar man.

David gives him twenty pounds.

"**Thank you. Here is eight pounds change,**" says the bar man. "**We will bring your meal to your table when it's ready. Salt, vinegar and sauces are on the counter, over there.**"

"**Thank you,**" says David.

He goes to the counter and takes some salt, vinegar, and sauce. Then, he sits down and drinks his beer. The beer is very smooth. He likes it very much. He looks around the pub. It is a very old pub, and there are old pictures of London on the walls. Some people are reading newspapers and drinking. Other people are eating lunch. The bar man brings his meal. He eats everything and then he orders another pint of beer. He has a very good time in the English pub!

10. BOOKING A TAXI

Today is Friday. David has been in London for a week. He is going back to Shanghai tomorrow.

He asks the receptionist to book him a taxi.

"Excuse me, could you book me a taxi to Heathrow, please?"

"Certainly, Mr Wang. What time do you need to be at the airport?"

"Well, my flight leaves at around one pm, so I need to be there by around ten am," says David.

"OK. I'll book a taxi for around eight thirty am," says the receptionist.

"Thank you very much," says David.

That evening, David packs his suitcase. It is very heavy. He looks at the photographs on his camera. He had a good time in London. He went sightseeing, he made a new friend, he went to the bank, he went shopping, and he spoke a lot of English. He also went to an English pub and drank English beer. He enjoyed his time in London. He feels very tired, so he goes to bed early. He dreams about his trip.

11. GOING TO THE AIRPORT

The next morning, he wakes up and looks at the clock. It says "8:15".

"Oh no! It is 8:15! I overslept! I am going to be late!" says David.

He jumps out of bed and gets dressed. He has no time for breakfast. He picks up his suitcase and bag and goes down to the reception desk. He gives the receptionist his key, and he checks out.

"Thank you for staying at our hotel, Mr Wang. Have a good flight," says the receptionist.

"Thank you," says David.

He gets in the taxi. There are many cars on the road. David is worried.

"Excuse me," he says to the driver. **"How long will it take to get to the airport?"**

"Well, the roads are very busy today, so it will take about an hour and a half," says the driver. **"What time is your flight?"**

"One o'clock," says David. **"But, I have to be at the airport by about ten o'clock."**

"Don't worry," says the driver. **"We will arrive at around ten o'clock."**

The taxi arrives at Heathrow Airport at ten o'clock. David goes to the check-in desk and checks-in.

12. CHECK IN AND DEPARTURE

"Hello, sir. Can I see your passport and ticket, please?" says the woman on the check-in desk.

"Here you are," says David.

"How many bags are you checking in today, sir?" asks the woman.

"Just one," says David.

"Please put it on the scales."

The weight limit for suitcases is 20kg. David puts his bag on the scales. It is 19.9kg!

"Would you like a window seat or an aisle seat?" asks the woman.

"A window seat, please," says David.

"OK, here is your boarding pass. Please check the screens for your gate number," says the woman.

"Thank you," says David. He goes through security and into the airport lounge. He is very hungry. He has breakfast at a café. Then, he waits for his flight in the lounge. After a few minutes, he looks at the screen.

"Go to gate."

David goes to the gate and waits.

After around fifteen minutes, he hears an announcement.

"We would like all passengers seated in rows thirty to forty to come to the gate for immediate boarding. All passengers seated in rows thirty to forty, please."

David looks at his seat number on his ticket. His seat is number thirty-two.

"That's me!" he says.

He gets on the plane. He closes his eyes and falls asleep. He dreams about his time in London. He had a very good time, and he hopes to visit London again in the future.

THANK YOU

Thank you for reading A Trip to London. (Word count: 4,714) We hope you enjoyed it. Other books in the Useful Phrases series are A Homestay in Auckland and A Business Trip to New York

There are quizzes about this book on our free study site I Talk You Talk Press EXTRA. http://italk-youtalk.com

If you would like to read more graded readers, please visit our website http://www.italkyoutalk.com

Other Level 1 graded readers include
A Business Trip to New York
A Homestay in Auckland
Dear Ellen
Haruna's Story Part 1
Haruna's Story Part 2
Haruna's Story Part 3
Ken's Story Part 1
Ken's Story Part 2
Life is Surprising!
Strange Stories
The Christmas Present
The Old Hospital
We Met Online

ABOUT THE AUTHOR

I Talk You Talk Press is a Japan-based publisher of language textbooks, graded readers and language learning/teaching resources.

Our team is made up of highly experienced language teachers and translators, who have all studied at least one additional language to an advanced level.

This experience enables us to design our materials from the perspective of both the teacher and the learner. We consult with both teachers and language learners when designing our textbooks and graded readers, and test our materials extensively in the classroom before publication.

We are a fast-growing press, and currently publish graded readers for learners of English. We publish new graded readers monthly.